All You Wanted

Diet &

Through Ayurveda

Vaidya Suresh Chaturvedi

New Dawn

NEW DAWN
a division of Sterling Publishers (P) Ltd.
A-59, Okhla Industrial Area, Phase-II, New Delhi-110020.
Tel: 26387070, 26386209; Fax: 91-11-26383788
E-mail: info@sterlingpublishers.com
www.sterlingpublishers.com

All You Wanted to Know about Diet & Health Through Ayurveda
© 2002, Sterling Publishers Private Limited
ISBN 81 207 2456 9
Reprint 2001, 2005

Published by Sterling Publishers Pvt. Ltd., New Delhi-110020.
Lasertypeset by Vikas Compographics New Delhi-110020.
Printed at Sai Early Learners Press (P) Ltd., New Delhi-110020.

Contents

Preface

According to Ayurveda, like human beings, plants and animals are also made up of five elements only. And being homologous, they form a part of human diet and meet the requirements of body tissues. *Anna* (food) is considered to be *prana* (life) yielding.

"प्राण: भृताम् अन्नं"

After getting assimilated, *anna* (food) facilitates the construction and preservation of normal vital components, namely, chyle, blood, flesh, fat, bones, bone marrow and semen. Their essence is termed as, and originates from, animals and plants and they nourish the brain and the heart.

There are eight requisites of food. They are — nature, material, additions, processing, quantum, time, eating place and eater.

The food taken as per the prescribed schedule is known as *yuktahara*. Its signs are—lightness in the belly and lack of any difficulty in breathing, circulation and other movements. Ideal food is digested early and it leads to contentment and normal excretions of urine and faeces. Mild belching indicates satisfaction after a *yuktahara*.

Nature of Food: One must take food according to the place, time, climate and one's own constitution and temperament.

An unsuitable or improper diet combination is claimed to be the producer of various diseases in both Ayurveda and Yoga. A balanced diet always helps in physiologic processes whereas an

6

imbalanced one leads to diseases. At one juncture, in the *Bhagvad Gita*, Lord Krishna says, "I am the digestive fire in living animals, and in altered forms of *prana* and *Apana Vayu*. I only devour all the four types of food, and get them digested." It is given in Ayurvedic texts that he who takes a balanced diet, does not succumb to diseases, always remains healthy and hearty, does not get infatuated with material pleasures, works according to proper reasoning, remains unbiased, veracious, merciful, kind and gentle to all.

युक्ताहारविहारस्य युक्तचेष्टस्य कर्मसु।
युक्तस्वप्नावबोधास्य योगो भवति दुःखहा।।
(गीता 6/17)

The *Bhagvad Gita* further says that yoga destroys all material pains for one who

7

regulates his food, amusements, sleep and work.

Moderation in eating, recreation, sleeping and other activities is the prescription that has been insisted upon, for yoga, by the Lord. Yoga is not possible for him who eats too much, nor for him who does eat nothing at all. Here the term 'eat' includes not only the process of consuming things through the mouth, it also includes the enjoyment gained through all the avenues of sense perceptions and inward experiences. Intelligent moderation is the law.

Proper Food: The food one eats depends upon the mental nature of a person. The food consumed also determines his nature.

The *Gita* says:

आहारस्त्वपि सर्वस्य त्रिविधो भवति प्रियः।
यज्ञस्तपस्तथा दानं तेषां भेदमिमं शृणु।।
(गीता 17/7)

There are differences in food preference, in forms of sacrifice, in austerity and charity according to the three modes of material nature. (Now hear of these).

In this context, Lord Krishna says, the temperamental influences that govern the mind and its thoughtful life express themselves in all departments of activity in which the individual employs himself. His choice of food, friends, the types of emotions in his bosom, and the view of life that he entertains, are all indicative of the type to which the seeker belongs.

Now read the following *slokas* of the *Bhagvad Gita*, in which we find enumerated

9

a series of symptoms, by which we can correctly classify ourselves.

आयुः सावबलारोग्यसुखप्रीतिविवर्धनाः ।
रस्याः स्निग्धाः स्थिरा हृद्या आहराः सात्त्विकप्रियाः ।।
(गीता 17/8)

Food dear to those in the modes of goodness increases the duration of life, purifies one's existence, gives strength, increases health, happiness and satisfaction. Such food is juicy, fatty, wholesome and pleasing to the heart. It is also conducive to a healthy body.

All the different types of food eaten by man in the world, have been classified and brought under four types on the basis of their physical properties. They are savoury, greasy, firm and cordial types of food.

10

Not only is our inner nature built by the type of food consumed, but the inner nature in its turn, commands our tastes.

कट्वम्ललवणात्युष्ण तीक्ष्णरुक्षविदाहिनः।
आहारा राजसस्येष्टा दुःखशोकामयप्रदाः।।

(गीता 17/9)

Food that is too bitter, too sour, too pungent, too dry or too hot, causes distress, misery and disease. Such food is very dear to those in the mode of passion.

Such a diet, no doubt, creates in an individual, brilliant energies, but in their wildness, they are, to a degree, uncontrollable and therefore, in their final reactions, they lead the eater towards a life of 'pain, grief and disease.'

यातयामं गतरसं पूति पर्यूषितं च यत्।
उच्छिष्टमपि चामेध्यं भोजनं तामसप्रियम्।।

(17/10)

Food prepared more than three hours before mealtime, which is tasteless, juiceless, and decomposed, besides having a bad smell and consisting of remnants and untouchable things, is very dear to those in the mode of darkness.

Thus we see that when the texture of thought changes, so does the taste and choice of food.

There is a saying in Ayurveda:

"रोगा: सर्वेऽपिजायन्ते मिथ्या आहारा विहारत:"

This means: eating the wrong food and engaging in wrong activities are the causes of diseases. All diseases grow out of improper food and improper engagement.

Therefore, everyone should be aware of proper food and its effects on the body, and also the results of imbalanced food. By the above references from the *Bhagvad Gita* and Ayurveda, we can say that, diet is one of the main factors which affects our health and gives birth to diseases.

Ayurvedic Concepts

Introduction

Ayurveda is one of the great gifts of the sages of ancient India. It is one of the oldest scientific medicinal systems in the world. It is also known as the Pancham Veda or the Fifth Veda, thus indicating its importance.

Ayurveda teaches us how to maintain and protect health, how to cure diseases and how to achieve longetivity. It is a science which deals with the principles and practices of the ways of healthy and happy living. It is believed that the human body materialises the human duties, activities and desires, and therefore, it is the duty of every individual to preserve it by the best possible means. But at the same time, one must keep in mind that the ultimate goal of human life is to achieve *moksha* i.e. salvation, and (for this reason) we are supposed to indulge only in good things.

According to Ayurveda, this universe has originated from the five elements — earth, water, fire, air and space.

These five elements constitute our body in various distinct and indistinct forms such as metabolic components (*dosha*), vital components (*dhatus*), and eliminable and products (*malas*).

The *doshas* are of three kind ie. *vata, pitta* and *kapha*. *Vata* is compossed of air and space, *pitta* of fire and *kapha* is the product of water and earth. The vital components (*dhatus*) are seven in number — chyle, blood, flesh, fat, bones, bone marrow and semen. And finally, the excretory components are of three kinds: faeces, urine and sweat.

Diet

Ayurvedic texts have a lot of details about diet and daily routine which help attain good health. Diet comes first among the three pillars of life which also include sleep and controlled sex.

Diet is the presentation of food articles arranged in quantity and quality, according to the needs of the body. It varies according to habit, climate, age and personal need. Foods are prepared out of natural substances, from the animal, the vegetable or the mineral kingdom. It is on account of 'food' that all living things grow.

Food is the origin of strength, life activities and the bright glow of the skin.

The appearance, health and strength of a person is due to intake of food according to its quality, quantity and variety. Diseases, and unsatisfactory health result from an unbalanced diet.

Importance of Diet
It is already mentioned that living beings, plants and all other distinct material things are made up of the five elements. Plants and animal parts are used as the diet of human beings to meet the requirements of body tissues. Food is considered to be life yielding.

Food taken passes down the oesophagus and proceeds through the stomach to the small and large intestines. This is known as *dhara*.

After getting assimilated, they facilitate the construction and preservation of

17

normal vital components of the body —
chyle, blood, flesh, fat, bones, bone marrow,
semen. Their essence is termed as *oja*, which
nourishes the brain and the heart.

Components and Tastes

All vegetable as well as non-vegetable
substances used in food or drug preparation,
should first be examined regarding their
particular utility on the touchstone of their
response to human tastes.

Ayurveda classifies six types of taste —
sweet, sour, salty, bitter, pungent and hot.
These are supposed to be the result of the
combination of the five elements
underlying the superficial phenomena of
the vegetable kingdom.

The whole world is the result of the
reciprocal combinations of these five
elements. Ayurvedists decide upon the

nature of the combination of whatever is found and responds to human taste in the vegetable and material kingdom. They have come to the conclusion that these six tastes are the combination of the five elements. The combinations are explained below:

1) The sweet taste is due to the combination of earth and water.

2) The sour taste is the combination of fire and earth.

3) The salt taste is also the result of the combination of fire and earth.

4) The bitter taste is due to the combination of space and air.

5) The hot taste is due to the combination of fire and air.

6) The pungent taste is the result of combination of earth and air.

Out of these tastes, the sweet, the bitter, the pungent and the hot and sour are generally found in the vegetable kingdom. The salt taste does not exist in it but is abundant in the seas and oceans.

Another speciality of the vegetable kingdom is that its tastes are mostly very distinct, while the tastes found in the material kingdom are more or less of mixed nature and are in most cases indistinct. There is also another conspicuous difference between the two. The tastes of the material kingdom are more or less fixed, while those of the living world are changing.

The sweet, sour, and hot are the three prevailing tastes in the fruit forms of the vegetable kingdom which serve as food.

20

The human body has a greater affinity towards the combination of earth and water — sweetness.

It appears that in the human body there is more storage of the earth and the fire components; the water and the air components are derived in smaller quantities from food materials but in larger quantities from the surrounding atmosphere. The balance is thus maintained.

After digestion, the substances of each of these gets converted into other substances suitable for our body. The taste of these new substances are said to be different, for instance, salty substances become sweet.

Properties

According to Ayurveda, each matter has twenty properties. The four main properties are:

(i) heaviness eg. Black gram

(ii) lightness eg. Green gram

(iii) cold eg. Sandlewood

(iv) hot eg. Brinjal.

The effect of substances taken as food in the body, may be pacifying or exciting, cold or hot. The sweet, the bitter and the pungent have cold efficacy. While the sour and the salt have hot efficacy.

A person should eat what is 'beneficial' and in appropriate and moderate proportion. It should also be taken at proper times. A disregard of this rule causes discomfort and diseases.

Beneficial food is a combination of food, which keeps a person in good health and helps to maintain the normal functioning of the body as a whole. At the same time, it corrects the irregularities of the body.

Beneficial Diet

Beneficial diet consists of those foods which after digestion, appear similar to the constituents of the body. Water, ghee, milk, rock salt, varieties of rice, wheat, barley etc., are very beneficial and promote health in all human beings.

But even out of these, the following are the best:

- Red variety of rice
- Mudga class of pulses
- Rainwater, collected from high above the ground
- Rock salt
- Cow ghee
- Cow milk
- Til oil

- Fat of the boar, taken from the animals living in a country where there is plenty of water and herbs
- The fat of a cock
- The semi-solid fat of goats
- Grapes
- Sugar

Ayurveda also says that:

- Food is the best sustainer of life
- Water is the best reviver of life
- Bathing is the best remover of exhaustion
- Milk is the best strengthener of life
- Flesh is the best fattener of beings
- Decoction of flesh is the best satisfier of hunger sensations
- Salt is the best provider of taste
- Vegetable acidity is the best strengthener of heart

- Honey is the best subduer of *kapha* and *pitta*
- Liquid ghee is the best subduer of *vata* and *pitta*
- Til oil is the best subduer of *vata*, as well as *kapha*
- Buffalo milk is the best to induce sleep
- Sugarcane is the best to increase urine
- Indian Gooseberry is the best to preserve youth

Consuming by way of habit, both milk and ghee, is very beneficial for old age.

Similarly, gargling with mustard oil is the best way to strengthen teeth.

Liquorice root is the best source of keeping active strength intact, eye-troubles out, and of ensuring sex-enjoyment, growth of hair, good voice, improved skin-hue, stoppage of menstrual secretion and maintenance of the rounded form of the body.

The Proportion of Food Intake

Food should be eaten in appropriate quantity. Too much or too little results in vitiation of all the three *doshas*. If inappropriate quantity of food is taken, it neither gets properly digested nor is it converted into faeces. If an inappropriate quantity of food undergoes digestion, it interferes with the maintenance of the body heat and causes diseases. One should eat only that amount of solid food which will occupy one-third space of the stomach, the next one-third should be filled with liquids and the remaining should be reserved for the generation of metabolic components.

Ayurveda advises that the proportion of food consumed by a person, should not cause — any uneasiness in his stomach; throw any reflex pressure on his heart; cause a visible expansion of his ribs; and make his stomach feel unusually heavy. Eating of the food should cast a pleasing influence on the action of the organs. It should only satisfy the hunger and the thirst, and not generate more thirst. On eating, the person should feel natural ease in carrying out his work, during his natural breathing or while laughing. He should allow his food to be digested in due time, and should find his strength and skin maintained by it.

When, however, food is taken in a quantity smaller or larger than necessary, the result will be lack of physical strength, a loss in brightness of the skin and a feeling of dissatisfaction. The person thereby reduces the length of his life, lowers his power of sex enjoyment and also the working capacity of his body, mind, intellect and of the various organs. He thus loses all the eight substantialties in point of his skin, blood, flesh, fat, bones, bone marrow, semen and health of mind. He appears wretched and renders himself liable to any one or more disease, due to the vitiation of the *vata dosha*. When the food is taken in excess, it causes vitiation of all the *doshas*. When a man takes plenty of solid food and drinks liquid to his heart's content, all the three metabolic components in his stomach get suddenly upset to an excessive degree. In their vitiation, they enter the undigested balance of the food and get locked in a part of the stomach, or begin to be thrown out as vomit or faeces.

Consumption

A person is supposed to be ready for his meal, when — he discharges his urine normally and has evacuated his bowels satisfactorily; his heart and feelings are buoyant; the three metabolic components are functioning normally; he belches in a healthy way; has a strong feeling of hunger and a clear flow of gases from his bowels; feels sure that his digestion is satisfactory and quick; all the organs work properly at their maximum capacity; and when his body feels light. He should then proceed to take his next meal.

Rules for Eating

A man should take his food while it is hot, with sufficient amount of ghee in it, in a pleasing place and with all supplementary requirements placed near by. Food should be eaten neither slowly nor too quickly. One should devote sufficient time for chewing each morsel of food before swallowing. One should neither talk or laugh unnecessarily during a meal, nor be absent-minded. While eating, a man should concentrate on the property and the preparation served to him for the maintenance of his health.

The food should be eaten after taking a bath, or at least after washing one's hands and feet. A person should then see that it has been offered to ancestors, gods and unknown quests. Children and old people in the house, and pet animals if any, should also be served first. If possible, friends and relatives should join him during his meals. The food should be served by beloved persons, in a pure condition of body and mind. While eating, the person should not criticise the food served. Attendants should see that it is full of all varieties of substantial food and is quite agreeable to him.

The sweet, fatty, nutritious and not quickly digestible food-substances, the solid substances, sweet fruits such as jack-fruit, mango etc. should be eaten at the beginning of the meal. Thereafter eat food that is salty and sour. Finally, all the easily digestable, fatless and hot substances should be eaten.

The Seasonal Adaptation

The vital importance of space and time has inherently been understood in ancient India. Time is catagorised as day and night, week, fortnight, month, season and year.

A person who knows the suitable diet and regimen for every season, and practices accordingly, has enhanced strength and lustre.

During winter, the digestive power of humans possessing good health is enhanced due to the restraint caused by the cold wind, so much so that it is capable of digesting any food, irrespective of its heaviness and quantity. When it does not get the proper fuel, the digestive fire affects the nutritive fluids resulting in the vitiation of *vata*, which has a cold quality. Therefore, during winter season, one should take greasy, sour and salt juices of the meat of fatty aquatic and marshy animals.

During the spring, the accumulated *kapha* which is liquefied by the heat of the sun, disturbs the power of digestion and causes many diseases. So, one should administer therapies like emesis, etc. and should avoid heavy, oily, sour and sweet diets. In this season, one should not sleep during the day time. At the advent of spring, one should habitually resort to exercise, unction (oil massage), gargling and collyrium.

During the summer, the sun evaporates the moisture of the earth. Thus the intake of sweet, cold, liquid and unctuous diets and drinks is prescribed. One should take cold *mantha* (a type of groat) along with sugar, as well as the meat of animals or birds of arid climate, ghee and milk with rice. One should not drink alcohol at all or drink in little quantity, along with plenty of water. One should also avoid taking food which is salty, sour, pungent or hot. Physical exercise is also to be given up during this season.

In the summer, the following foods are beneficial:

Grains: Barley, white millet, great millet, old rice and wheat.

Vegetables: Spinach, dill, fenugreek, pointed gourd, bitter gourd.

Legumes: Red gram, green gram, lentil, bengal gram, pea, horse gram, marble pea.

Meat: Goat, dry roasted fish, small fish, crabs, lobsters, prawns, rabbits, partridge.

Tubers: Garlic, ginger, onion, carrot, radish, turmeric.

Fruits: Papaya, vegetable-marrow, watermelon, musk melon.

Milk products such as butter-milk, butter.

Spices: Clove, cumin seeds, black pepper, asafoetida, mustard, honey, dried seeds and fresh leaves of coriander.

Water: Ginger water, sandalwood water, sago water, honey water, katha water.

The following food however should be avoided:

Grains: New rice

Vegetables: Lady's finger

Legumes: Black gram

Meat: Pig, big fish, duck, buffalo, bullock.

Tubers: Potato, beetroot, amorphophallus, tapioca.

Fruits: Banana, guava, custard apple, cucumber, peach, strawberry, watermelon, walnut, pista, cashew-nut, orange, hog plum, India jujube, palmyra palm fruit.

Milk: Curd, curd mixed with water, ice-cream, cheese, cottage cheese, cream, dry sugar-free condensed milk.

Fried food, sweets, sesame, cold water should also be avoided in summer.

In the winter season, the following foods are beneficial.

Grains: Maize, rice, great millet.

Vegetables: Bottle gourd, lady's finger, snake gourd, fenugreek, red pumpkin, spinach, cabbage, cauliflower.

Legumes: Black gram, marble pea, green gram.

Meat: Goat, rabbit, deer, hen, duck, pig, fish, prawn, lobster.

Tubers: Amorphophallus, arum, carrot, ginger, beetroot, onion, sweet potato, potato, tapioca.

Fruits: Grapes, apple, walnut, fresh date, dried date, apricot, dried black grape, coconut, orange, sapota, melon lime, Indian jujube, kabith, Indian berry (*Greuria subinequalis*), pineapple.

Milk: Curd, ghee, milk, butter, dry sugar-free condensed milk, cottage cheese, cheese, cream, butter-milk.

Besides these, sweets, sugar, sesame, clove, cashew-nut, almond, pistachio, tomato and warm water are also beneficial.

In the winter season, the following foods should be avoided.

Grains: White millet, pearl millet, ragi, barley, old grains.

Vegetables: Fenugreek, sun flower, drumstick, bitter gourd, dill, brinjal.

Legumes: Lentil, hyacinth bean, pea, gram, horse gram, dewbean.

Meat: Dry, smoked, roasted meat and small fish.

Tubers: Radish, garlic.

Fruits: Banana, guava, custard apple, palmyra palm, black plum, tinned-fruit, papaya.

Poppyseed, cumin seed, chilli, fried food, cinnamon and cold water should also be avoided in winter.

Some Cures and Benefits

Milk

Milk is one of the most common items of food throughout the world. It occupies a unique position in the maintenance of health and healing diseases.

The milk of cow, buffalo and goat is generally used. Cow's milk contains almost twice as much protein as human milk, but less sugar. Buffalo's milk contains more fat than cow's milk.

Milk is regarded as a complete food. It contains protein, fat, carbohydrates, vitamins, minerals and all the food ingredients considered essential for sustaining life and maintaining health. The protein from milk is of the highest biological value and it contains all the amino-acids essential for body-building and repair of body-cells.

Milk increases the strength and resistance power, improves memory and removes exhaustion. Milk is highly beneficial in weight gaining. Cows' milk is useful in hyperacidity. Milk is very useful in curing insomnia. It acts as a tonic and tranquiliser. Milk is also useful as a cosmetic and beauty aid. It is beneficial in the treatment of fever, tuberculosis and anaemia, urinary tract infection, leprosy, fatigue, and tiredness. Hot milk taken at night acts as a laxative.

Food Value:

Moisture – 87.5%, protein – 3.2%, fat – 4.1%, minerals – 0.89%, and 4.4% carbohydrate.

Minerals and Vitamins:

Calcium – 120 mg., phosphorous – 90 mg., iron – 0.2 mg., small amounts of vitamin B-complex, K and P. Calorific Value – 67.

Curd

English Name - Yogurt

Indian name - Dahi

Curd or yogurt is a lactic fermentation of milk. It is preferred for its pleasant and refreshing taste. It is highly health promoting. Curd is a very nourishing food, a valuable source of proteins, essential vitamins and minerals. It is also a rich source of calcium and riboflavin. It is useful in chronic constipation and diarrhoea, colitis, chronic appendicitis and gastric ulcer.

Curd is valuable in the treatment of insomnia. The patient should take plenty of curd and massage it on the head. This will induce sleep.

Curd is a full diet in itself. We take curd or various forms of curd in our daily meal. Curd can also be utilised as a home remedy.

It is beneficial in hepatitis, burning in the rectum and skin disorders.

Internal Use

1. Cooling Effect: Chilled curd mixed with water gives freshness in case of excess body heat, physical and mental weakness and giddiness.

2. Memory Enhancement: One cup of curd with 2 teaspoon of sugar, twice a day, smoothens body roughness and strengthens memory.

3. Nausea: In nausea and vomiting, curd with ½ tea spoon of ground mint leaves is helpful.

42

External Use

1) Hair Fall: To stop hair fall and to make hair soft and thick, massage curd gently on scalp and wash it off once a week.

2) Black Spot on Skin: In case of skin diseases, roughness or black spots, massage curd on the body before bath. It clears the skin.

3) Pimples: Apply cream of curd gently on pimples before bath.

4) Boils/Acne: Keep curd in a bronze pot for a week, daily stir copper in it. When the curd becomes green in colour, apply it as ointment on the boil/acne.

Caution

In case of cough, cold, fever, asthma, body-swelling, fracture and injury, curd should be avoided.

Food Value

Moisture – 89.1%, protein – 3.1%, fat – 4.0%, minerals – 0.8%, carbohydrates – 3.0%.

Minerals and Vitamins

Calcium – 149 mg., phosphorus – 93 mg., iron – 0.2mg., vitamin A – 102 I.U., vitamin C – 1mg., small amount of vitamin B-complex, Calorific Value – 60.

Butter

When curd is churned with water and fat is removed, that fat is called butter.

It is used in general debility to strengthen the body. Butter is curative of burning sensation of any type. It is useful in nerve strengthening and in eye diseases.

Butter-Milk

When curd is churned with water and fat is removed, the residual is called butter-milk. It is useful in strengthening muscles. It is an appetiser in *vata*-related diseases.

In *kapha*-related diseases, add a pinch of dry ginger powder and black pepper in butter-milk. In *pitta*-disorder add sugar in it.

Butter-milk with little water and coriander leaves, taken twice a day, ends burning micturation.

Add a pinch of asafoetida, roasted cumin seeds and rock salt in butter-milk. It is very useful in gaseous disorder, piles, diarrhoea, abdominal pain, amoebic dysentery, anaemia and liver disorder. In gout, joint pain, arthritis, rheumatoid arthritis, cold and cough, butter-milk should be avoided.

Ghee

Clarified butter or ghee is not necessarily a fermented product. It is prepared in many ways. Consumption of ghee removes the dryness of body. It softens the skin and brings glow to the face. It also strengthens muscles and bones. It is useful in the treatment of bodyache, pain in the joints and various other *vata*-related disorders.

However ghee contains cholesterol. Excessive consumption of ghee hence results in thickening of arteries, leading to heart diseases.

Cheese

Cheese is an unfermented milk product but cheese produced commercially, in the West, is a fermented product. There are over 400 varieties of cheese.

Cheese contains some or all of the fat from milk, besides vitamin A, calcium, phosphorus, thiamine and riboflavin. It strengthens the muscles. It is a nervine tonic and is also useful in skin disorders.

Sugar

Sugar is made from sugarcane. It is also made from beet, carrot and sweet potato.

Sugar is useful in quenching thirst, and in curing eye disorders and general debility. One pinch of salt and sugar with water is very effective in diarrhoea, dysentery and dehydration. Sugar and sour lime, added to a glass of cold water, make a very pleasant drink on a hot day. It is a good source of energy and provides relief in fatigue and vomiting. Syrup made of sugar is an excellent preservative for fruits and jams.

Excessive use of sugar is harmful for our body as it causes diabetes and tooth decay in children.

Sugarcane

Botanical name : Saccharum officinarum

Hindi name : Ganna

Sugarcane is an important plant with a metabolism leading to the accumulation of sucrose. It is transported as glucose and fructose within the growing plant. The juice of sugarcane is nutritious and refreshing. It contains about 15% natural sugar and is rich in organic salts and vitamins.

It strengthens the heart, kidney, eyes, brain and sex organs. It is sweet and cool and diuretic. It also acts as an aphrodisiac.

It is useful in excessive thirst, fever, jaundice, scanty urination, burning micturation, gonorrhoea, enlarged prostate, cystis and nephritis. In abdominal distention, eye disorders, hiccough and epistaxis sugarcane is very useful.

Jaggery

Jaggery is produced by heating sugarcane juice. It is reputed to be a heart tonic. It is hot in nature. It strengthens muscles, acts as an aphrodisiac and a diuretic. It is highly beneficial in migraine. 10 gm. jaggery, mixed with 5 gm. ghee and taken early in the morning is very helpful for migraine.

It is a digestive stimulant. Jaggery is useful in bodyache, arthritis and other *vata* disorders.

Honey

Honey is a popular, amber coloured, sweet and thick liquid, available throughout the world.

Its utility is described in Hindu and various other religious literatures, both as a requisite for rituals and or as a medicine.

It is made by honeybees and is obtained from their combs. There are many varieties of honey according to the trees and flowers in the surrounding area of the honeycomb.

Honey is used in various forms in every house. It is used in diet and medicine, and can be taken throughout one's life.

Honey has numerous medicinal values.

Internal Use

1. Throat Infection: In throat congestion, take ½ teaspoon of honey thrice a day.
2. Memory Enhancement: Those who have a weak memory, should take one teaspoon of honey with one cup of milk to strengthen the memory.
3. Bright Complexion: To clear the complexion, one teaspoon of honey with ½ teaspoon of lemon juice, taken twice a day, is very helpful.

4. Tonic: Honey acts as an energiser if a person takes it daily with bread, toast or chapati.

5. Abdominal Complaints: One teaspoon of honey with the powder of 2 cardamoms, taken thrice a day, is very useful in hiccups, abdominal heat, giddiness, excessive thirst, vomiting, piles and excess bile.

6. Cough and cold: To get relief in cough and cold, take one teaspoon of honey with 10 drops of finger or betel leaf juice, thrice a day.

7. Obesity: Obesity has today become a curse for both children and adults. To reduce it, children should take one teaspoon of honey with a glass of water, early in the morning, upto three months. For adults, one tablespoon of honey

with a glass of water, as above, is prescribed for as long as necessary.

External use

1. To heal a wound or injury, honey can be applied as an ointment or antiseptic.
2. Persons who have weak eyesight, or who are suffering from any eye problem, should apply honey in the eyes with absolutely clean eye liner brush every night. This improves the eyes.

Cereals and Pulses

Grains like wheat, rice and pulses, have been given a very special place in Ayurvedic literature. It is said that within grains, there is life and it is with grains only that life persists. Given below are some details of various cereals and pulses.

Wheat

Botanical name : Triticum aestivum

Wheat is the most common cereal in our daily food. It is also readily available. In a normal diet, the various products made from wheat and wheat flour play an important role. Wheat is sweet in taste and cold in nature. It is slightly heavy for digestion, but at the same time, it strengthens the body and its regular use increases all the vital components of the body.

Wheat products can be consumed in many ways. It can be had as *dalia* which is nothing but coarsely ground pieces of wheat, cooked in milk or water. *Dalia* mixed with ghee, if boiled with milk and sugar, is an ideal breakfast, especially for growing children. Also, *chapati* can be prepared out of wheat flour; it is very easy to digest, while *puri*, which is the same thing deep-fried in ghee or oil, is heavy.

Wheat is beneficial in various diseases when generalised weakness is a main symptom. In such conditions, wheat, in the form of *sheera* (wheat cooked with sugar and dry-fruits), if taken regularly with milk, strengthens the body. It is also beneficial for diabetic patients. *Chapati* made out of wheat flour without oil or ghee, if served to diabetic patients, is very beneficial. It strengthens and retains the stamina of the body.

In case of abscesses, or broken bones, wheat flour mixed with turmeric and water, if applied in the form of 'poltis', helps a lot.

Rice

Botanical name : Oryza sativa

Rice forms an important component of our diet. It is sweet in taste and cold in nature. It subdues acidity. Rice too is light and easy to digest.

The consumption of rice increases enzymes, components of blood, muscles and other elements of the body. It is owing to rice that the body remains light and energetic. Different preparations made out of rice are used in the diet. Rice boiled in milk with sugar, is very good for growing children. *Chidwa*, made out of rice, is also very easy to digest. It is also consumed in the form of *idli* and *dosa*.

Uses in Different Diseases

Rice and rice products are used in the treatment of constipation, fever, diarrhoea, dysentery, abdominal complaints and emaciation. Normally old rice is more in use than the recently grown ones because of its special qualities.

In case of leucorrhoea or micturation, rice starch (water) is especially beneficial.

Great millet

Botanical name : Sorghum bicolor
Hindi name : Jowar

Great millet is also a common cereal in our diet. It is sweet in taste and cold in nature.

Usually *chapatis* made out of this flour are used.

Uses in Different Diseases

Great millet, as it reduces the heat in the body, is useful in *pitta*-related diseases. It is very easy to digest and useful in curing abdominal diseases. It strengthens the body and increases sexual potency.

Flour made out of its shallow fried grains, if mixed with milk, ghee and sugar, proves to be a very beneficial breakfast, especially for small children and old people.

Also for diabetic patients, *chapatis* made out of this flour is beneficial.

Barley

Botanical name : Hordeum vulgare

Barley is cold in nature. It stimulates the digestive system and makes one alert.

Regular use of barley helps to rule out obesity by reducing the fat. It is also useful in increasing intelligence and memory. As barley is cold in nature, it helps in many urinary tract diseases. It also helps in skin diseases.

Barely is useful in the treatment of common cold, fever and sore throat.

Shallow fried barley, which is very dry in nature, helps in case of obesity.

Pearl millet

Botanical name : Penniselum americanum

Hindi name : Bajra

Pearl millet is sweet in taste and hot in nature. It is commonly used in the form of *chapati*. It is very useful for body-building. Its consumption strengthens the body and forms all the elements of the body in the right proportions.

It is specially useful in winter when appetite is increased.

It is good for people suffering from arthritis, diabetes and obesity. It is also useful in chronic constipation, as it has a high-fibre content. For lactating mothers, *chapatis* made out of pearl millet are very useful, as it is very good for milk secretion.

Bengal gram

Botanical name : Cicer arietinum

Hindi name : Chana

Bengal gram can be used in three forms:

1) Whole grain
2) Pulses
3) Gram flour

Bengal gram is sweet in taste and is heavy for digestion. It increases *vata* in the body. A fist-full of grams, soaked overnight and tied in a cloth, will stimulate sprouting. Sprouts are very nourishing.

Pulses and gram flour improve health, give strength and stimulate sexual potency. Gram flour is beneficial in case of constipation.

Red gram

Botanical name : Cajanus cajan

Hindi name : Arhar

Red gram is commonly used in India. It is sweet in taste, easy to digest and helps in the formation of stool besides being useful in *pitta*-related diseases.

If taken regularly, it improves of complexion. In case of small children, water of the boiled dal is very nourishing.

Green gram

Botanical name : Vigna radiatia

Hindi name : Mung

Green gram is green in colour and small and round in shape. After grinding, it breaks into two pieces and thus is transformed to *dal*. It is used in three forms:

1) Grain
2) Pulses with the peel
3) Pulses without the peel

Green gram is very easy to digest. It is cold in nature and useful in eliminating *pitta*, and thus helps to ease burning sensations of the body and stomach.

Pulses with the peel is especially beneficial in eye diseases. In any type of fever, use of green gram in the diet is very beneficial as it helps in reducing body temperature. It stimulates digestion and increases appetite. It is also used in diseases of the digestive system such as diarrhoea, dysentery, colitis, etc.

Black gram

Botanical name : Vigna mungo

Hindi name : Urad

Black gram is round in shape and black in colour. It is also used in three forms :

1) Grain
2) Pulses with the peel
3) Pulses without the peel

It is heavy for digestion but at the same time, it increases the appetite. It is useful in treating various diseases causes by *vata*. It increases muscle strength and sexual potency of the consumer. Regular use of this is helpful in increasing the sperm count, hence can be used in cases of male infertility.

It cures constipation and therefore is especially beneficial in case of piles.

Lentil

Botanical name : Lens culinaris

Hindi name : Masoor

It is a round-shaped grain. It can be used as whole gram or dal without the peel.

Lentil is very easy to digest and helps in the formation of faeces. It increases *vata* in the body. It is also useful in *pitta* and *pitta*-related diseases. It thus cures blood and skin diseases. As it is cool in nature, it should be avoided in arthritis and chronic cough and cold.

In case of all types of fever, its use in the diet is especially beneficial.

Oil and Oil-Seeds

The presence of some sort of oil/fat in our diet is also essential. This can be obtained from milk and various oil seeds. Different types of oils are used in different regions of our country.

Sesame

Botanical name : Sesamum indicum
Hindi name : Til

According to Ayurveda, oil obtained out of sesame seeds has the best medicinal value. Consumption of white and black sesame seeds increases strength, eliminates worm infestation in the intestine and strengthens the roots of hair, thereby making them healthy. It also increases appetite and is useful in increasing milk production in lactating mothers. It is also useful in cleansing of the womb after pregnancy. Besides, it is used in treating complaints like polyurea.

In rheumatic or rheumatoid arthritis as well as in many *vata* diseases, use of sesame oil internally, is very beneficial. Proper massage with this oil is especially beneficial for skin, hair and eyes.

Mustard

Botanical name : Brassica juncea

Mustard seed is a well-known oil seed. It is a small annual plant which grows upto a height of one metre, with some branches.

It is hot in nature according to Ayurveda. Mustard seed as well as its oil is used for the treatment of various ailments. Mustard oil boiled with *heena* leaves, is useful in healthy growth of hair. Mustard seeds have emetic properties. They are especially useful in drunkenness, narcotic and other poisonings. They are also beneficial in muscular pain, convulsion in children, ringworm, constipation and abdominal disorders.

This oil is mainly consumed in the north-eastern region of India. It is sticky in nature and has a very strong odour. It increases appetite. Being hot in nature, its consumption brings about the elimination of *kapha* and *vata*-related disorders. It also eliminates worm infestation from the intestine. Regular use of this oil in the diet, helps in reducing the excessive fat of the body. A massage of the body with this oil removes dryness of the skin, makes it soft and smooth and strengthens the muscles.

Groundnut

Botanical name : Arachis hypogaea

Groundnut oil is also commonly used in the diet. It subsides *vata* and is especially beneficial in many diseases. But at times it increases acidity in the body, and its use is contraindicated in skin diseases.

Coconut

Botanical name : Cocos nucifera

Coconut oil is easily digested and is therefore used for cooking and frying. It is extensively used in the preparation of vegetable ghee. It is also useful in coconut cake. It increases the quantity and nutritive value of milk if given to cows.

Coconut oil is useful in skin diseases and is beneficial for healing wounds.

Vegetables

Ash gourd

Botancial name : Benincasa hispida

Hindi name : Kohla

Ash gourd, generally referred to as *hara petha* in India, is a round whitish-green fruit. It is used as a vegetable as well as in sweetmeats. It tastes sweetish and is easily digestible. It is refrigerant in action and hence useful in summer. It is a good appetiser and is also used as a light food during illnesses associated with heat.

For making sweetmeat, its pieces are boiled in concentrated sugar solution. This sweet, known as *petha* is cool in nature and a promotor of vital components of the body.

It is therefore a good nutritious food supplement.

As medicine, it is useful in heart diseases and mental aberrations. Those who suffer from headaches during summer and those exposed to mental tension, can be advised to consume ash gourd. Since it has got antacid and anti-bilious properties, it is beneficial to people suffering from hyperacidity, heartburn and vomiting.

It should be avoided in all rheumatic diseases, paralysis, sinusitis, common cold, diabetes and obesity.

Garlic

Botanical name : Allium sativum

Garlic is a stimulant and a digestive and it cures gas and constipation.

1) One piece of garlic crushed and boiled in one cup of water, reduced to half a

cup, is filtered and mixed with a pinch of salt, and taken as tea. This decoction is useful in malaria.

2) In sudden fall of temperature, garlic juice should be rubbed all over the body, palms and soles.

3) Gastric troubles are footed out by the daily use of its chutney.

4) One piece of garlic boiled in one cup of milk, till it is reduced to half, is useful in rheumatic arthritis, sciatica, back pain and paralysis.

5) It is useful in painful menses and improves eyesight and voice.

6) In enlargement of spleen, two pieces of garlic, crushed and used with one glass of butter-milk twice daily, is useful.

7) Regular use of garlic in any form controls blood pressure, heart disease and blood cholesterol.

8) Two drops of garlic juice dropped in the nostrils is effective in epilepsy and hysteria.

9) Its juice is useful in earache.

10) Regular use of garlic, improves blood circulation and cures chronic cold and cough, gives relief in dry piles and hiccups.

11) For infants suffering from cough and cold, apply garlic paste over chest and back. It gives instant relief.

12) It can be used as a paste in fracture, eczema, ringworm and dog bite.

Garlic must be avoided in diabetes, gout, vomiting and pregnancy.

Potato

Botanical name: Solanum tuberosum.

Potato is the most popular and widely used vegetable in the world. It is an annual plant,

71

producing swollen underground stem tuber. This vegetable forms an indispensable item of daily food and is an important source of nutrition.

It is useful in intestinal toxemia, uric acid diseases, renal calculi (stones), dropsy, scurvy, inflammation, rheumatism and skin blemishes. The juice of raw potatoes, is very valuable in clearing skin blemishes as an external application.

Potato can be consumed in various forms such as baked and steamed or in soups. It strengthens the muscles.

It is cold in nature, so it should be avoided in cough and cold, epileptic conditions, improper digestion, arthritic conditions, obesity and diabetes.

Bitter gourd

Botanical name: Monordica charantia
Hindi name: Karela

The bitter gourd is a common vegetable, cultivated extensively all over India. It is green in colour, long, tapering at the ends and covered with blunt tubercles. The seeds are white in the raw fruit and become red when they ripen.

It acts as an antipyretic, appetiser and laxative. It is hot in nature. It is useful in diabetes, piles, blood disorders like boils, scabies, itching, psoriasis, ringworm and other fungal diseases, fever, jaundice, worm infestation, rheumatoid arthritis and gout disorders.

Amorphophallus

Botanical name: Amorphophallus campanulatus

Hindi name: Suran

It is a round-shaped root. It is often used as an appetiser. It is highly beneficial in piles and in splenomegaly. It should be avoided in skin diseases like itching, ringworm and leprosy.

Brinjal

Botanical name: Solanum melongena

It is oval-shaped, violet, green or white in colour. According to Ayurveda, its nature is hot, so that it should not be consumed in blood disorders and skin diseases. It can be had in diseases like arthritis, obesity and diabetes. It is also a sexual stimulant.

Beans

Beans are of many types. They are green in colour, along with seeds. They are heavy for digestion. They strengthen the muscles and aggravate the fats. They can be consumed in all seasons, except rainy season, as they are heavy for digestion.

Bottle gourd

Botanical name: Lagenaria siceraria
Hindi name: Lauki

Bottle gourd is a common vegetable in India. It is whitish-green in colour, having the shape of a bottle. It has white pulp with white seeds embedded in spongy flesh.

It is sweet and easily digested. It strengthens the body and is also an aphrodisiac. It is useful in gynaecological disorders, urinary tract infection and habitual abortion. It is highly beneficial in fever, diarrhoea, asthma, heart and eye diseases. It subsides *pitta* and so it is beneficial for hyperacidity.

Spinach

Botanical name : Spinacia oleracea

Spinach is a leafy vegetable with broad-green leaves. The leaves are cool in nature and very nutritive. It is demulcent, diuretic and laxative.

Spinach is an excellent food remedy for constipation. It is a valuable source of high-grade iron and vitamin A. It is useful in anaemia and night blindness.

Spinach juice is effective in strengthening gums, preventing and curing dental cavities and pyorrhoea. A mixture of carrot and spinach juice, taken early in the morning, can cure bleeding and ulcerated gums. It is the richest source of folic acid. It is highly beneficial in pregnancy and lactation, in urinary, respiratory and gaseous disorder, in fever, acidity and colitis. Spinach is often cooked as a vegetable used in soups and salads. It is also mixed with other vegetables and pulses.

Amaranth

Botanical name: Amaranthus gangeticas
Hindi name: Chaulai ka Sag

Amaranth is a popular green leafy vegetable grown all over India. It is usually a short-lived annual plant. It is sweet and cold, so it is helpful for relieving body heat. It has useful stimulant and digestive powers. Regular use of amaranth in the diet prevents deficiency of vitamins A, B, B2 and C, calcium, iron and potassium. It protects against several disorders such as defective vision, respiratory disorder, recurrent colds, retarded growth and functional sterility.

It is a very good blood purifier, useful in anaemia, abdominal disorders, constipation, amoebic dysentery, gynaecological and liver disorders, splenomegaly, long-standing fever, pregnancy and lactation, retarded growth, premature ageing, bleeding tendencies and leucorrhoea. It is also a very good diuretic.

Fenugreek

Botanical name: Trigonella foenum-graecum
Hindi name: Methi
Fenugreek is a well-known leafy vegetable. Regular consumption helps keep the body healthy.

Fenugreek is an annual herb. It has compound leaves of light-green colour and thin pointed pods. The seeds are brownish yellow and emit a peculiar odour. It is bitter in taste but not in nature. It improves appetite. It is useful in the treatment of digestion, flatulence, sluggish liver, colic disorder, dysentery, diarrhoea, dyspepsia and worm infestation. The leaves help in blood formation. So it is valuable in anaemia, pregnancy and lactation.

It should be avoided in burning sensation, hypertension, vertigo, menorrhagia, bleeding piles and skin diseases.

Cucumber

Botanical name: Cucumis sativus

Cucumber is a very popular and widely cultivated vegetable in India. It gives a cooling and refreshing effect. It contains almost all the essential elements needed for health.

There are several varieties of cucumber, which differ in shape, size and colour. The best vareity is fresh, firm, smooth, regular in shape, and dark green in colour.

It is useful in *pitta*-related diseases. It is naturally diuretic and highly beneficial in the treatment of burning sensation in urinary calculus, stone in the kidney or bladder, excessive thirst, abdominal distention, indigestion, general debility, constipation and skin eruptions. It is also effective as a beauty aid and is the best tonic for the face. Its regular use prevents pimples, blackheads, wrinkles and dryness of the face.

Radish

Botanical name: Raphanus sativus
Radish is one of the most commonly used vegetables in India. It is a hairy annual herb.

It has only one root which is long and tapering. It stimulates appetite and promotes a healthy bloodstream.

Radish is one of the richest sources of iron, calcium and sodium.

The leaves of radish are diuretic and laxative. The root is very helpful in preventing and curing scurvy and the seeds are expectorant carminative for relieving gastric discomforts.

The juice of the fresh roots are regarded as an effective food remedy in piles. The juice is also beneficial in the treatment of dysuria, painful inflammation, severe urethral pain and cystitis. It is useful in jaundice. The paste made from the seeds of the radish is valuable in leucoderma. Radish seeds contain a bleaching substance and emulsion of the seeds with water, applied all over the face, will remove black heads and freckles.

Beetroot

Botanical name: Beta vulgaris

Hindi name: Chukander

The red beet, commonly known as garden beet, is a juicy root vegetable.

The vegetable is a good tonic for health. It contains carbohydrates, mainly in the form of sugar, and a little protein and fat.

Beets are of great therapeutic value. They clean the kidneys and gall bladder. Red beet juice has blood forming qualities due to its high content of iron. It regenerates and reactivates the red blood cells, supplies fresh oxygen to the body and helps the normal function of vesicular breathing. It is extremely useful in the treatment of anaemia.

The juice of the red beet strengthens the body's power. Beetroot destroys *vata* and diseases arising from the formulation of *vata*. It is also useful in *kapha*-related diseases.

Beet juice is beneficial in the treatment of jaundice, hepatitis, constipation and piles. The celluloid content of one beetroot acts as a bulk residue and increases peristalsis. It is valuable in the treatment of hypertension, arteriosclerosis, heart trouble and varicose veins. It is beneficial in skin disorders like boils, pimples and pustules.

Cabbage

Botanical name: Brassica oleracia

Cabbage is one of the most highly-rated leafy vegetable. It is excellent as a muscle builder and cleanser.

Raw cabbage salad is an excellent remedy for constipation. It is useful in duodenal ulcers and obesity. One of its most valuable contents, tartaric acid, inhibits the conversion of sugar and other carbohydrates into fat. Hence it is of great value in weight reduction.

It is beneficial in skin disorders like ulcers, infected sores, blisters and skin eruptions, including psoriasis.

Cabbage contains several elements and factors which enhance the immunity of the human body, and arrest its premature ageing. They prevent the formation of patches on the walls of blood vessels and stones in the gall bladder.

Sponge gourd

Botanical name: Luffa cylindrica
Hindi name: Tori

It increases milk in lactating mothers. It is an aphrodisiac. It relieves abdominal pain, distention and flatulence. It is very useful in preventing worm infestation and piles. It is also beneficial in gynaecological disorders.

Coriander

Botanical name: Coriandrum sativum

It improves the taste of food. It is useful in indigestion, piles, worm infestation, dysentery and emaciation. It is very good for curing hyperacidity. It can be safely consumed in bleeding disorders like menorrhagia, piles, pimples and other skin disorders.

Mint

Botanical name: Mentha spicata

Mint contains a lot of vitamins and is rich in several minerals.

Mint oil is used in chewing-gum, in toothpastes and in confectionary and pharmaceutical preparations. Mint is a carminative which relieves gastric discomforts. It also acts as a stimulant, relieves muscle strain and improves appetite.

It is good for liver, kidney and bladder. It is beneficial in colic, thread worms, morning sickness and summer diarrhoea.

Fresh leaves of mint, chewed daily, is an effective antiseptic. It strengthens the gums, prevents tooth decay, and pyorrhoea. It also keeps the mouth fresh and gives a good taste to the tongue.

Gargling fresh mint decoction with salt cures hoarseness caused by shouting or singing loudly. Application of fresh mint juice over face every night cures pimples and prevents dryness of the skin. It is useful in natural birth control.

Onion

Botanical name: Allium cepa

The onion is a pungent edible root vegetable. It is available in two colours white and red. It has been used as a food remedy. It is useful for stimulating digestive power. It also acts as an expectorant and a diuretic. It is useful in fever, epileptic and hysterical attacks, sunstroke, tooth disorders, anaemia, sexual debility, ear disorders, urinary tract infections, retention of urine, bleeding, piles, etc.

Ginger

Botanical name: Zingiber officinale

Ginger is a perennial herb with underground branching stems called rhizomes.

Ginger should be taken regularly in case of indigestion, gastric trouble and loss of appetite. Headaches can be cured by squeezing two drops of ginger juice into the ears. Fever acompanied by cold can be hastened to a speedy cure by the intake of ginger tea, twice or thrice a day. Chronic cases of diarrhoea and dysentery can be helped by the intake of one gram of ginger mixed with a quarter gram of rock salt in cold water. For cough, half a spoonful of ginger juice mixed with honey and half a spoonful of betel leaf juice, gives quick relief.

It is used as a spice and a medicine. Ginger is a valuable drug for disorders of the digestive system. It is extremely useful in dyspepsia, flatulence, colic, vomiting, spasms and other painful stomach disorders. It is an excellent remedy for cough and cold and other respiratory disorders. It is useful in menstrual disorders like dysmenorrhoea and amenorrhoea.

Tomato

Botanical name: Lycopersicon-esculentum

Tomato is one of the most important vegetables throughout world.

When it is raw, it is green in colour and after ripening, it becomes red.

It is a digestive stimulant. It increases haemoglobin percentage and hence is useful in anaemia.

Tomato juice is one of the most widely used juices. It is useful in amoebic dysentery, diabetes, general debility and U.T.I. (Urinary Tract Infection). Being a rich source of vitamin A, tomatoes prevent night blindness and other eye problems caused by the deficiency of the vitamins. Tomatoes are highly beneficial in the treatment of obesity. A glass of fresh tomato juice mixed with a pinch of salt and pepper, taken in the morning, is considered an effective remedy for morning sickness, billiousness, liver disorder, jaundice, indigestion and burning sensation in the chest due to hiatus hernia. It is contraindicated in, oedema, joint pain, kidney stone, nephrites, pharyngitis or laryngitis.

Soyabean

Botanical name: Glycine max

Soyabean is one of the most nutritious foods, with seeds more or less round and yellow, green, brown or black in colour. It is a valuable source of proteins, vitamins, minerals and other food ingredients. It is useful in diabetes, skin disorders and anaemia. It improves the complexion, stimulates growth and relieves constipation.

Soyabeans are used in other forms such as flour, bean sprouts, soyabean milk and oil.

Turnip

Botanical name: Brassica campestris

Hindi name: Shalgam

Turnip is a type of root vegetable. It is available in many colours like red, green and white. It is sweet in taste. It is the richest source of vitamins. It is a digestive stimulant. It is useful in *vata* and *kapha* disorders. It is a laxative and improves blood circulation of the body and is helpful in heat diseases. It is useful in strengthening muscles, and toning up the body.

Fruits

Lemon

Botanical name: Citrus limon

It is a very popular citrus fruit which constitutes a very important item and plays a significant role in our daily diet, because of its nutritional and vitamin C rich qualities.

According to modern scientists, it is rich in sodium phosphorus and chlorine which are essential ingredients for the healthy growth of our body. It also contains protein, fat, sugar, and vitamins B and C in sufficient quantities. These are indispensable for our body and its healthy growth.

Lemon can be used in various ways according to one's necessity.

Internal Uses

1) Obesity : Two tablespoon of lemon juice mixed in a glass of luke-warm water if consumed daily, reduces fat.

2) Gastric Trouble: Two spoonfuls of lemon juice, mixed with a pinch of black rock salt in a glass of water, gives alertness to the person throughout the day and also protects him from many gastric troubles and ailments.

3) Nausea: One spoon of lemon juice with two spoonfuls of sugar, duly mixed in a glass of water, stops nausea, vomiting, giddiness and burning sensation in the body. It also quenches thirst.

4) Liver diseases: Lemon juice, if taken along with meals, goes a long way in curing various liver ailments. Half-pieces of lemon, sprinkled with salt and

black pepper-powder and made a little hot on fire, should be sucked slowly. It gives prompt relief to all stomach-diseases and gastric troubles.

External Uses

1) Lemon juice, milk and gram flour paste proves useful in skin diseases like black spots and pimples.
2) One or three drops of well-filtered lemon juice in eyes, cures eye-sores and ophthalmic troubles.
3) Cut-up lemon should be rubbed on the scalp in case of baldness and dandruff.
4) Lice are killed by applying lemon juice mixed with garlic to hair.
5) Lemon juice mixed with water, if gargled, removes bad smell and cures mouth ulcers.

6) Worms and other germs are killed if enema of lemon juice with water is taken.
7) Lemon juice mixed with pre-boiled (raw) milk acts as the best cleansing agent for face.

Mango

Botanical name: Mangifera indica

The taste of mango is sweet, palatable and tasty. So everybody likes it. Mangos are used in varied ways and in different preparations.

Raw Mango

This will stimulate the appetite and saliva. Boiled mango juice with sugar/jaggery is useful in sunstroke and nausea. It proves useful in enlargement of spleen.

Ripe Mango

This should be soaked in water for about two hours before eating, or kept in the refrigerator. Mango juice taken in its original form is light and improves the digestive system. It also increases blood circulation.

General Uses

1) Mango with milk is always useful and very palatable, and it increases blood formation and blood circulation. It also improves the nervous system and tones up the muscles.

2) One cup of milk, after taking mangoes, strengthens the muscles.

3) Continuous use of mangoes for a certain period, cures diarrhoea, dysentery, liver disorder, chronic stomach and intestinal diseases, tuberculosis and piles.

4) Regular use of mango is very useful for gaining weight and body development.

5) The mango is enriched with proteins and vitamins A and B. It is a heart-tonic and also increases sexual strength. It brightens the skin and makes the face smooth and fresh.

6) Mango *papad* is useful in belching and vomiting. It is very easy to prepare mango *papad*. Spread mango juice over a piece of cloth or over a metal plate in size and shape as required, and let it dry under the sun. The resultant wafer is mango *papad*.

Mango, if consumed in excess, will create several diseases namely indigestion, slow appetite, blood disease, heaviness in the abdomen and gastric trouble. Those suffering from fever, cold, cough, asthma and diarrhoea should avoid consumption of mango.

Grapes

Botanical name: Vitis vinifera

Grapes are used as remedy in many diseases. Daily intake of grapes gives lustre and smoothness to skin, removes giddiness and recoups blood. For infants, 1 to 2 tablespoons of grape juice at night brings easy motion.

Internal Use

1) Eat 25 gm (a handful) of grapes before going to bed and have a glass of hot milk over it. It proves very useful in preventing constipation.

2) Daily use of grapes and milk is useful in weakness, giddiness and nervousness.

3) Take 10 grapes, boil in one cup of water, and when reduced to half, filter it and take twice a day for curing painful menstruation.

4) One ounce of grape juice mixed with a little sugar and water, subdues thirst and cures indigestion and stomatitis.

5) Soak 10 to 20 grapes at night in a cup of water. Crush it, discard the pulp, mix a little sugar and take it in the morning. This reduces abdominal heat.

6) One cup of grape juice early in the morning is useful in curing migraine and headache due to mental tension. In chronic conditions, you can add a little coriander juice in it. It is a rich diet in fever. Warm up 5 to 10 raisins, add salt and black pepper in it. It helps in nausea and belching.

7) In dry cough, warm some raisins on the flame, sprinkle a little salt and black pepper over it and chew it.

8) Soak 10 to 25 raisins at night, squeeze it in the morning, filter it and drink it. This juice helps to remove eye burning and urine trouble.

Orange

Botanical name: Citrus reticulata

Orange is a juicy and very delicious fruit obtained from small trees. It is considered highly energetic on account of its cooling and soothing actions on the body. Taken as a medicine, it may cure many day-to-day health problems.

Internal Uses

1) Consumed regularly, orange brings back lost appetite, fights against indigestion and other gastro-intestinal troubles.

2) Orange juice mixed with salt and black pepper powder, helps in checking biliary disorders, nausea, anorexia, flatulence and belching. It is also good for anaemic people.

3) The fruit as such, taken after meals, corrects indigestion and brings lightness in the abdomen. It is a good nourishment for the body and the mind.

4) It forms an ideal part of the diet during pregnancy and also helps in alleviating high blood pressure and associated symptoms.

5) In infants it helps in healthy dentition and keeps them fit.

External Uses

Dried orange peels, crushed and ground into a thin paste with rosewater and applied over the face, removes pimples and improves complexion. It also removes black patches of sunburn. This is to be applied in the morning, before bath.

Banana

Botanical name: Musa paradisiaca

Banana is an all season fruit found all over India, especially in the coastal regions. Many varieties of this fruit, having different tastes, effects and appearances are available.

Ripe banana is quite delicious and a good appetiser, vitaliser and makes a complete diet in itself. Banana can be used in loose motion and dysentery, to control and compensate fluid and electrolytic loss. Dried banana wafers, dusted with salt and pepper powder, are good appetisers.

Fresh juice collected from banana stem, curbs the thirst produced in choleric-dehydration. At the same time it also curbs heamatemesis, allergic disorders like urticaria, chronic cough etc.

It is curative of U.T.I. like retention of urine or change in colour and consistency of urine. As a tonic, fresh banana taken along with milk, is supposed to have rejuvenating and aphrodisiac effects. Banana shake in combination with cardamom helps in chronic cough.

Precautions

Banana should not be taken on an empty stomach since it may lead to abdominal complaints. Unripe bananas may also have similar effect.

Guava

Botanical name: Psidium guajava

Guava is cultivated all over India. It is sweet or sour in taste. It is valuable for

104

maintaining health and strengthening the body. It is very useful in heart diseases, burning sensation of the body, dysentery, vertigo, fatigue, typhoid, worm infestation, and abdominal pain. In migraine, raw guava paste, applied on the forehead early in the morning, is very helpful. Guava consumed daily helps to build up body strength and keep away diseases.

Apple

Botanial name: Malus pumila

Apple is a sub-acid fruit and one of the most valuable of all the fruits. It is a fleshy fruit with tough skin, ranging in colour from greenish-yellow to red and has pinkish or yellowish-white flesh. Apart from its energy value, it plays an important role in the normal development of metabolic functions, that is, the chemical and physical changes that takes place within the body and enable its continual growth and functioning.

Apple is a highly nutritive food. It contains minerals and vitamins in abundance. The skin of the apple should not be discarded while eating as the skin contains more vitamin C than the inner flesh.

Apples are valuable in the maintenance of good health. Apples being rich in iron are highly beneficial in the treatment of anaemia. They are useful in constipation, amoebic-dysentery, headache, heart disease, hypertension, rheumatic affection, dry cough, piles, kidney stones, splenomegaly, eye disorders, skin and dental disorders. It promotes vigour and vitality. It also increases digestive power and has aphrodisiac qualities. It is a rejuvenator.

Fig

Botanical name: Ficus glomerata
Hindi name: Anjeer

Fig occupies a high position among fruits. A fig is soft, sweet, pulpy, delicious and promotes health. It is also available in dry forms.

It is beneficial in general debility, removes physical and mental exertion and endows the body with renewed vigour and strength. It is an excellent tonic for weak people. It is useful in constipation, piles, asthma, cough, oliguria, liver disorder, jaundice and sexual debility. It is also a blood purifier.

Zizyphus

Botanical name: Ziziphus jujuba
Hindi name: Ber

Zizyphus is liked and consumed by all. It is useful in fever, bowel disturbance, burning sensation of the body, burning micturation and U.T.I. It is beneficial in reducing excessive thirst and is very useful in improving sex stamina.

Lime

Botanical name: Citrus aurantifolia

Lime is an important fruit of the citrus group. It is very popular in the tropics and is used as a necessary adjunct to everyday meals. It is regarded as a health-building food of great value.

There are many varieties of lime, differing in size, colour and shape.

Lime juice forms an indispensable ingredient of salads. It is mixed with cooked pulses, soups, sauces and gravies to make them more tasty and palatable. Lime is used in various diseases of bones and joints. The vitamin C content in lime increases the body's resistance to disease. It is also helpful in maintaining the health of teeth and other bones of the body. It prevents decay and loosening of the teeth, toothache, bleeding of the gums and fragility of bones, thus minimising the rate of osteoporosis.

Lime is considered highly beneficial in the treatment of digestive disorders. A teaspoon full of fresh lime should be mixed with black pepper and taken as a medicine.

In indigestion, a small lime should be slit into two, sprinkled with black pepper, heated and sucked.

In case of nausea, have a teaspoon of lime juice mixed with jaggery. In cholera, lime juice mixed with hot water should be taken.

Lime pickle is useful in abdominal pain. Lime juice is also excellent for weight reduction. Fresh juice of a lime, mixed in a glassful of water and sweetened with honey, should be taken every morning on an empty stomach in case of obesity.

Lime acts as a blood purifier. It can be used as a beauty aid. A fresh lime squeezed in a fully boiled glass of whole milk, with a teaspoon of glycerin in it should be left for half an hour and then applied on the face, hands and feet before retiring at night. This application every night will help in depigmentation, removing freckles and dryness of the skin, and make you look young and beautiful. Massaging the scalp with a few drops of lime juice mixed with amla powder before going to bed, stops falling of hair, lengthens it and prevents premature greying. It also cures dandruff.

Papaya

Botanical name: Carica papaya

Papaya has been regarded as one of the most valuable of tropical fruits. It is large, fleshy, hollow, cylindrical or pear-shaped.

The fruit has a thin smooth skin. It is dark green in colour when raw but as the papaya ripens, it changes to bright-yellowish. It has a delicate aroma and a delicious flavour.

Ripe papaya is an excellent tonic for growing children and nursing mothers. It provides energy and body-building materials. Papain, a digestive enzyme in the raw papaya, is highly beneficial in the deficiency of gastric juice and excess of unhealthy mucus in the stomach. It corrects habitual constipation and bleeding piles. Papaya is a powerful destroyer of helminth roundworms.

It is beneficial in skin disorders. A paste of the papaya seeds is applied in skin diseases like ringworm. It is also used in cirrhosis of liver, throat disorder and splenomegaly.

Rose apple

Botanical name: Sizygium jambos

Hindi name: Jamun

Rose apple is a well-known common fruit. The fruit is a juicy berry with a single seed. It is black outside and violet inside, has a sourish-sweet pulp and greenish-yellow seed. It is cultivated in the Indo-Malyasian region.

It is highly beneficial in diabetes, polyuria, diarrhoea, dysentery, piles, liver disorders like hepatomegaly, and in female sterility.

Coconut

Botanical name: Cocos nucifera

Coconut contains almost all the essential nutrients needed by the human body. It is also considered a sacred fruit.

The outermost part of the fruit is green and shining when tender. It becomes rough after maturity. It is almost entirely water-proof and very hard. The inside of the fruit is soft, milky-white and fresh. The cavity grid in the flesh is filled with a watery fluid.

Coconut is a nourishing, strengthening and fattening diet.

It can be taken with vegetables, salads and also cooked as a green vegetable.

The water of the tender, green coconut, is mineral water. It is cooling and useful in excessive thirst, diarrhoea, U.T.I., cholera, urinary disorder, worm infestation, infant vomiting, abdominal pain, migraine and acidity.

Pineapple

Botanical name: Ananus comosus

Pineapple is very tasty and sweet. It is useful for the heart. It is beneficial in heat stroke, indigestion, acidity, worm infestation, fever, diptheria and anasarca, excessive thirst and general debility.

Pear

Botanical name: Pyrus communis

Hindi name: Nashpati

Pear is a sweet and tasty fruit. It is useful in strengthening the body. It is beneficial in amoebic dysentry in children, excessive thirst, vomiting, chronic constipation, loss of appetite and indigestion. Regular consumption of pear acts as an aphrodisiac.

Plum

Botanical name: Prunes domestica

Hindi name: Aaloo bukhara

Plum is a juicy fruit and red in colour. It is cultivated in the Himalayas in the Tarai region. It is sour in taste but ripened plum tastes very sweet.

It is useful in bodyache, joint pain, *vata*-related disorders, excessive thirst, nausea, constipation and diabetes. It is highly beneficial in jaundice or hepatitis.

Wood apple

Botanical name: Feronia limoria
Hindi name: Kaith
Wood apple is useful in hiccups, asthma, earache, worm infestation and bowel and digestive disorders in children.

Pomegranate

Botanical name: Punica granatum
Hindi name: Anar
Pomegranate is a very delicious and semi-seedy fruit. It has refreshing and soothing qualities and is more easy to digest than any other fruit.

All parts of the pomegranate tree has medicinal value.

It is good for treating inflammation of the stomach and pain of the heart. The juice from the fresh fruit is an excellent cooling beverage for thirst in case of fever and sickness. It increases the body's resistance against infections, particularly tuberculosis.

Pomegranate juice is of great value in digestive disorders. It is an appetiser. It is useful in vomiting, morning sickness, colitis, flatulence, diarrhoea, dysentery, intestinal worm, kidney and bladder stone, teeth and gum disorder, burning sensation of eyes, fever and burning micturation.

Musk melon

Botanical name: Cucumis melo
Hindi name: Kharbooja

Musk melon stops burning sensation of skin. It reduces excessive thirst. It is useful in insanity and in ideal development of neurons of the brain.

Watermelon

Botanical name: Citrullus vulgaris

Water melon is a big, green, tough skinned, fruit. After cutting, it is reddish and fleshy with blackish seeds. It is sweet and cold in nature. Useful in burning micturation and gynaecological disorders, it reduces body heat and acts as a tranquiliser and calming agent.

Litchi

Botanical name: Litchi chinensis

Litchi is very nourishing. It acts as a blood purifier. It is useful in weakness due to long standing illness. Litchi strengthens the digestive system. Litchi juice is useful in U.T.I. It is beneficial for regulating heartbeat

and improves the general resistance power
of the body.

Fresh date

Botanical name: Phoenix dactylifera

Date is one of the most nourishing fruits. It
is included in the categories of both dry and
fresh fruits. It is a very good tonic. Being
easily digested, it is very useful for
supplying energy. It is an excellent remedy
for intestinal disturbances and constipation.
Fresh date is highly beneficial in alcoholic-
intoxication, weak-heart, anaemia, sexual
debility, headache, and children's diseases
like diarrhoea and dysentery during
teething.

Dried dates

In diarrhoea, it is used in paste form. It is a
very good sex tonic. For sex stimulation it

should be consumed as follows: it should be boiled in milk at night, chewed slowly. The milk is to be drink separately.

Sapota
Botanical name: Manilkera achras
Hindi name: Chiku
Sapota is used as an ideal food during illness, as it promotes strength and gives energy. It is beneficial in cold and cough. It can be used in all types of climate throughout the year and by all age groups.

Custard apple
Botanical name: Annona squámosa
Hindi name: Sharifa
Custard apple is a sweet, delicious, fleshy and seedy fruit. It has cooling effects, reduces body heat and burning sensation of urine.

It is beneficial in thirst, dyspepsia, anaemia and vomiting. It strengthens the muscles and helps in weight gain. Excessive use of custard apple results in cough and cold.

The dried seeds of this fruit powdered and mixed in water, if applied on scalp daily for 10 mins. before bath, helps to get rid of lice and nits.

Almond

Botanical name: Prunus amygdlus

Almond is a highly nutritious food. It is an effective health-building food, both for the body and mind and a valuable food remedy for several common ailments.

It reduces cough. It is highly beneficial for increasing energy. It helps in the formation of new blood cells and haemoglobin, and plays a major role in maintaining the smooth physiological functions of brain, nerves, bones, heart and liver. Almonds boost the vitality of the brain and strengthen muscles for a prolonged life.

Paste of almonds with milk-cream and fresh rose buds, applied daily over the face, is a very effective beauty aid. It softens, bleaches and nourishes the skin. It also prevents wrinkles, black heads, pimples, dryness of the skin and keeps the face fresh.

Almond oil is beneficial in falling hair, premature graying, thinning of hair, constipation, skin disorders, and anaemia.

Walnut

Botanical name: Juglans regia

It is highly nutritious. It is useful in skin disorders and nervous debility. It strengthens sexual power and the body as a whole. It is rich in almost all the elements needed by the body.

Pistachio

Botanical name: Pistacia vera

Pistachio is one of the best nuts and seed foods. It strengthens the muscles and plays a major role in maintaining the smooth physiological functioning of brain, nerves, bones, heart and liver. It is useful during vomiting, cough, diarrhoea and stomatitis.

Raisin

Botanical name: Vitis vinifera

Raisins are dried grapes. All grapes are however, not suitable for making raisins. Only the grapes which are very sweet are selected for drying. Raisins have high nourishing qualities.

Raisins are extensively used in salads. They may be added to curries. They are also used in bakeries and confectionaries in the preparation of jams, jellies, cakes, puddings and pies.

It is useful in general debility, convalescence, constipation, anaemia, underweight and febrile condition. Black raisins are used for restoration of sexual vigour.

Spices

Ayurveda has described all the spices as cooking ingredients which have great therapeutic and taste value, whether taken singly or in combination. In diet they increase the utility, taste and acceptability of food. They have medicinal properties as well, and keep one healthy by preventing as well as curing many diseases.

One of the most common cooking ingredients, salt, for example, has amazing therapeutic value. Ayurvedic science has always been aware of this fact.

Salt

Salt is mainly used to add flavour to food. There are 5 types of salt:

1. Epsom salt
2. Common salt
3. Fruit salt
4. Black salt
5. Rock salt

Among these, epsom salt is considered to be the best and is normally used for medicinal purposes. It is however, too expensive for ordinary cooking. In cases of slight temperature, drink a cup of water boiled with a quarter spoon of epsom salt. Within a short time, the fever will come down. In cases of high fever, keep a piece of cloth soaked in epsom salt water over the forehead. The fever will abate after sometime.

Congestion in the chest can be relieved by drinking epsom salt water. It also alleviates suffering in cases of rheumatism.

For minor ailments such as stomachaches, indigestion and gas trouble, chewing a piece of epsom salt gives welcome relief. Relief is also obtained in cases of cough, sore throat and dental diseases by gargling with a cup of hot water mixed with a quarter spoon of epsom salt. In the case of dental problems, massaging the gums with this salt, mixed with mustard oil, also helps. In the absence of toothpaste, a quarter spoon of epsom salt mixed with 3-4 drops of mustard oil, can be used to clean the teeth. It is very beneficial.

Turmeric

Botanical name: Curcuma longa

Turmeric is useful in rheumatism and phlegm. It helps in skin diseases, diabetes and diseases related to blood. It stimulates the spleen. If there is a cut in any part of the body, turmeric powder (dried or in paste form) should be applied and lightly bandaged. In cough or cold, drinking a glass of hot milk mixed with half to one gram of turmeric powder, will work wonders. One should take the mixture for fifteen days, depending upon the gravity of the situation. However, not more than half a gram of turmeric powder should be taken during summer. For asthma, half a gram of turmeric powder mixed with two grams of jaggery, should be taken thrice a day. This medicine also soothes hiccups.

Complaints of cold or an overgrowth of nasal bone can be cured by breathing the smoke of turmeric powder. Roll some turmeric in a small piece of cloth like a cigarette and light one end of it. The smoke can be breathed by one nostril, while keeping the other one closed with the thumb. Or in a small vessel with a narrow mouth, put a few lighted pieces of charcoal and sprinkle turmeric powder over it. Bring the mouth of the vessel close to the nose and inhale. In cases of leucorrhoea, take a glass of hot milk with one gram of turmeric powder every day. It is advisable for diabetics to take half a gram of turmeric powder, mixed with one gram of sesame seeds and two grams of jaggery, in the morning and evening.

Asafoetida

Botanical name: Ferula asafoetida

Those suffering from gastritis should add a pinch of asafoetida to the food regularly. In case of high fever, if the body temperature drops suddenly, it is advisable to mix asafoetida in water and rub its thick paste on the palms and soles of the foot. If a child is suffering from stomachache, rub its stomach with asafoetida paste. Cases of indigestion and overeating can be alleviated by a small quantity of roasted asafoetida mixed with some black salt in lukewarm water. In the case of a venomous sting, apply the paste of asafoetida mixed in the sap of swallow-wort.

Cumin seed

Botanical name: Cuminun cyminum

It helps in increasing appetite and in the production of bile. It is antiphlegmatic and useful for the eyes. It also improves memory and cures gastritis and indigestion. It gives quick relief in cases of nausea and diarrhoea. Its decoction helps

130

in the contraction of the womb and stimulates lactic organs after childbirth. If menstrual flow is low, take one or two grams of cumin seed powder in fresh water, twice of thrice a day. Make a thick paste of cumin seeds and water and apply it on swollen hands and legs for an effective cure. Acute indigestion can sometimes cause nausea. Immediate relief can be obtained by taking one gram of cumin seeds with salt and water. Mix the paste in a glass of water in such proportion that the taste is not bitter. In cases of chronic indigestion, roast and grind cumin seeds and take one gram of it, in curd, twice or thrice daily, for 15-30 days or as long as the condition persists. Burning sensation in the chest can be alleviated by the intake of one gram of cumin seeds mixed with two grams of sugar. In case of fever, prepare a powder of cumin seeds and take one gram of it, mixed with two grams of jaggery, twice or thrice a day.

Thyme

Botanical name: Carum copticum
Hindi name: Ajwain

For the cleansing of the womb after delivery, drink the extract of one spoon of thyme, boiled in a cup of water, twice or thrice a day. It is beneficial to take thyme mixed with a bit of salt for stomachache, loss of appetite, indigestion, overeating and diarrhoea. For constipation, chewing one gram of dry thyme before going to sleep, will clear the bowels by the morning. It also kills worms present in the liver. Severe fever accompanied by cold can be cured with one gram of thyme powder taken twice or thrice a day. When a severe attack of asthma occurs, a spoonful of thyme decoction in a cup of water provides relief.

Dry ginger

The daily intake of dry ginger increases appetite and helps in cases of stomach disorder, rheumatism and nausea.

Half a teaspoon of dry ginger added to a cup of hot milk, is useful in cold and expectorant coughs.

One gram of dry ginger powder mixed in hot milk and taken in the morning and evening, proves beneficial in case of bodyaches, headaches and jointaches.

Clove

Botanical name: Eugenia caryophyllus
Cloves have been proved to help in treatment of slight fever, influenza, chronic cold, vomiting during pregnancy and toothache.

Powdered cloves if taken with rock salt, helps in flatulence. Apply ground cloves mixed with water on abdomen, in case of flatulence. In case of vomiting during pregnancy, cloves should be sucked with sugar. In case of low grade fever, one gram of clove powder can be given thrice a day with lukewarm water or honey. Clove oil, when mixed with sugar, is good in cold. Clove is also very good in case of dry cough. Clove oil instantly relieves toothache and helps in case of toothcavities. A paste of clove if applied on forehead, relieves headache.

Aniseed

Botanical name: Pimpinella anisum

Hindi name: Saunf

Aniseeds are useful in the treatment of stomachache, piles, constipation, nausea and vomiting.

Chew a teaspoon of roasted aniseed for stomachache. Powder of aniseed, if taken with lukewarm water at bedtime, gives relief in chronic constipation.

To improve appetite, roasted aniseed has to be taken with a pinch of black salt or common salt. It is very helpful in cases of vomiting and nausea and it decreases thirst. Cold syrup of aniseed helps in cooling the body, especially in summer. Powdered aniseed taken with water, twice a day, can cure piles. It is also good for heart patients.

Cardamom

Botanical name: Elettaria cardamomum

Cardamom is derived from the seed of the plant, Elettaria cardamomum. It has an aggreeable flavour and is used in cooking. Many chew cardamom after a meal or eat it with betel leaf. Cardamom has

135

carminative properties. It is useful in fever, flatulence, nausea, cough with mucus, weak eyesight and ulcers.

Black pepper

Botanical name: Piper nigrum

Black pepper is the dried fruit of the plant, Piper nigrum. White pepper is prepared by soaking black pepper and rubbing it to remove the outer cover. To obtain the best flavour, pepper should be freshly ground. Pepper is added either during cooking or at the table along with salt. Pepper added to hot tea has been endorsed as the best remedy for common cold.

Black pepper is highly beneficial in heart diseases, flatulence, abdominal distention, worm infestation, abdominal pain, dyspepsia, piles, and amoebic-dysentery. It is also useful in cholera, common cold, hiccups. 500mg pepper powder with honey in divided doses is very helpful in such cases.

In case of a sty, it is rubbed with water and applied on the affected part. It is powdered, added to warm water and used for gargling to cure expectoration of cough and hoarseness of voice. To improve weak memory, crush five pepper-corns in one teaspoon of butter, add candy, mix with milk and drink early in the morning.

Nutmeg

Botanical name: Myristica fragrans
Hindi name: Jaiphal

Nutmeg is the dried kernel derived from the seed of the tree, Myristica fragrans. It is used as a flavouring agent and also consumed as a carminative. It is beneficial for children suffering from common cold, pneumonia and influenza. Rubbed with water, mixed with honey and taken in 3 divided doses, it is useful in vomiting and diarrhoea. A thin paste of nutmeg powder can be applied on the forehead to relieve headache. It is useful in toothache, throat infection, soreness of throat, hypertension, weakness of heart and lung.

External application of paste of nutmeg with milk on face, helps to clean up black marks and pimples. It also improves complexion.

Cinnamon

Botanical name: Cinnamomum zeylaricum
Cinnamon is the dried, brown-inner bark of the tree Cinnamomum zeylaricum. It acts as a carminative. It is useful in soreness of throat, hoarseness of the voice, cough and asthma.

It is a digestive stimulant, useful in abdominal distention, flatulence, cholera, diarrhoea, amoebic dysentery, abdominal pain, headache, influenza.

Bayleaf

Botanical name: Cinnamomum tamala
Hindi name: Tejpatta

The leaf is dried and used in food as a spice. It is pungent. It is useful in cough, cold, asthma, and is a very good appetite stimulant. It is also used for abdominal distention, flatulence, dyspepsia, bodyache, joints pain, abdominal pain, weak uterus muscles and fever.

Betel Leaf

Betel leaf is popular in India as well as other countries and is well-known by the name *paan*.

In India it is considered auspicious. Betel leaf along with betel nut, is used in every religious and traditional occasion like, marriage, naming ceremony etc. In Hindu religious books it is stated to be the favourite of gods and goddesses. Before starting any religious function, betel leaf and betel nut is to be worshipped first.

Apart from this, betel leaf is commonly used for eating purpose. It is chewed for its pleasant taste. There are different varieties of betel leaves, like *banarasi*, *deshi*, *calcutta*, *poona*, *mahoba*, etc. They all differ in taste according to their properties, climate and place.

Betel leaf is popular with everybody. People in villages keep betel leaves at home and take it daily applying limewater, *katha* and betel nut. In cities, people go out to the shops to buy a special betel leaf preparation containing many ingredients.

According to Indian tradition, betel leaf should always be served after meals.

Betel leaf has a pleasant effect and it imparts a red colour to the mouth and lips.

It is a good appetiser, digestive, nutritious haematic and anti-depressant. It stops bad breath, improves complexion, blood circulation, vigour and vitality. It produces lightness in the body. It also improves digestion, increases gastric secretion and improves liver function.

Medicinal Uses

Betel leaf is used in various diseases.

- In common cold, cough, asthma, rhinitis, pharyngitis and laryngitis, its juice taken with honey, twice a day, is helpful.
- Betel leaf with clove and *mulethi* powder thrice a day, acts as antitussive in cough.
- With ginger and clove, it can be used to cure loss of appetite, pain and worms in the abdomen.
- In feeble pulse and low heartbeat, one teaspoon of betel leaf juice with half teaspoon of sugar twice a day, is helpful.
- The above combination is also useful in nervousness and depression.
- In filariasis, betel leaf with salt and warm water, twice a day, is helpful. Chewing of betel leaves with cardamom stops bad breath.

- Betel leaf juice with saffron and honey, improves blood circulation in people having cold and numb extremeties.
- Betel leaf with peppermint acts as an anti emetic.

External Uses

- In conjunctivitis, a mixture of honey and betel leaf juice, in equal proportion, is used as eye drops.
- In enlargement of gland and swelling, formentation with warm betel leaves is helpful.
- In headaches, warm betel leaves tied on the temple region gives relief.
- On abcesses, application of betel leaf is beneficial.
- In chest congestion and pain, application of warm betel leaf with oil, helps to bring out cough.

- For toothache, its juice applied with cotton or by finger is helpful.

Precaution

Betel leaves should not be taken in excess.

Betel leaves ingested in excess has its own bad effects like poor appetite, dimness of vision and deafness. It caused staining of teeth, tooth decay and stomatitis. It also causes hyperacidity.

It should be avoided by people having teeth problem, loose motion, conjunctivitis, giddiness, swelling, tuberculosis and haemophilia. Betel leaves should not be consumed by small children, pregnant women, alcohol drinkers, people suffering from pleurisy, urinary diseases and stomatitis.

After chewing betel leaf, the mouth should be washed properly before going to bed, so as to prevent tooth problem.

Diet Instructions for Specific Diseases

Obesity

Food to Eat

Grain : Wheat, barley, great millet, pearl millet

Pulses : Green gram, lentil, red gram, bengal gram

Vegetable : Radish, spinach, amaranth, bottle gourd, sponge gourd, roasted brinjal

Fruit : Papaya, sweet lemon, orange, rose apple, fig

Drinks : Hot water, barley water, coconut water, butter-milk, and lime water.

Roasted grains, pungent things should especially be taken.

Food to Avoid

Grain	: Rice
Pulses	: Black gram and dry red beans
Vegetables	: Potato, lady's finger, turnip, beans, peas, carrot, sweet potato, colocasia, and amorphophallus
Fruits	: Mango, grapes, apple, banana, pear, guava, sapota
Dry-Fruits	: Almond, walnut, cashew-nut and dates
Drinks	: Milk and milk products

Overeating, oily preparation, spices, meat, fish, sugarcane, sugarcane juice and its products and sweet dishes should be especially avoided.

Do not drink too much water along with the food.

146

Diabetes

Food to Eat

Grains : Wheat, barley, great millet, pearl millet

Pulse : Green gram, red gram

Vegetables : Radish, spinach, cabbage, fenugreek, lady's finger, cucumber, bitter gourd, leafy vegetables

Fruits : Rose apple, papaya, fig, apple, pomegrante

Drinks : Hot water, butter-milk, lime water, barley water

Leafy vegetables, triphala are especially beneficial.

Food to Avoid

Grains : New rice, new grains

Pulses : Black gram

Vegetables	:	Potato, cauliflower, sweet potato, beetroot
Fruits	:	Banana, mango, sugarcane, lime, sweet lime, grapes, sapota
Drinks	:	Lassi, alcohol, curd
Sleep	:	Completely avoid day sleep

Liver disorders

Food to Eat

Grain	:	Rice, great millet
Pulses	:	Green gram, lentil, red gram
Vegetables	:	Bitter gourd, bottle gourd
Fruits	:	Banana, coconut, lime, apple, grapes, pomegranate, sapota, pineapple

Coconut water and sugarcane juice are especially beneficial.

Food to Avoid

Grains   : Maize, pearl millet

Pulses   : Bengal gram, black gram

Vegetables : Potato, cauliflower, brinjal,
               radish

Fruits   : Papaya, guava, rose apple,
               mango

Drinks   : Curd mixed with water,
               butter-milk, coffee, tea

Fried, hot and spicy food, meat, fish should
be avoided.

Skin disorder

Food to Eat

Grain   : Old rice

Pulse   : Green gram

Vegetables : Bitter gourd, bottle gourd,
               ash gourd, drum stick

Fruits	:	Apples, grapes, sweet lime sapota
Drinks	:	Warm water

Sandalwood application, triphala and honey are beneficial.

Food to Avoid

Pulses	:	Black gram
Oil Seed	:	Sesame
Vegetables		Brinjal, tomato, cauliflower
Fruits	:	Sour fruits, lime, tamarind, dry fruits
Drinks	:	Butter-milk

Sweets made out of jaggery, pickle, garlic, hot and spicy food should be avoided.

Asthma

Food to Eat

Grains	:	Great millet, pearl millet, wheat

Pulses   : Green gram, lentil, red gram
Vegetables : Bitter gourd, fenugreek,
              spinach
Drinks   : Hot water, goat's milk
Ginger, dry ginger, butter, ghee are
beneficial.

Food to Avoid

Pulses   : Black gram, bengal gram
Vegetables : Tomato, radish, potato
Fruits   : Guava, orange, sweet lime,
              rose apple
Drinks   : Cold water, cold and sour
              things

Stomach disorders

Food to Eat

Grains   : Great millet, pearl millet,
              wheat

Pulses	: Green gram, lentil, red gram
Vegetables	: Bottle gourd, sponge gourd, tomato, radish, spinach, bitter gourd, cabbage
Fruits	: Pomegranate, grapes, sapota, apple, papaya, sweet lime, rose apple, orange
Drinks	: Hot water, rice-malt, cow's milk

Thyme, cumin seeds, coriander, pepper, aniseeds are beneficial.

Food to Avoid

Pulse	: Bengal gram , black gram
Vegetables	: Brinjal, cauliflower, lady's finger, tomato, potato, cluster beans, colocasia, sweet potato
Fruits	: Banana, mango, betel nut, zizyphus

Hot and spicy food, heavy food, jaggery should be avoided.

Arthritis/Gout

Food to Eat

Grains   : Wheat, maize, great millet

Oil Seeds   : Sesame

Vegetables   : Brinjal, fenugreek, snake gourd, drumstick, cabbage, bitter gourd, amaranth

Fruits   : Mango, apple, papaya, pear, grapes, sapota, rose apple

Drinks   : Milk, rice-water, tea, coffee

Garlic, ginger, dry ginger, butter, ghee, vegetable oils, and jaggery are beneficial.

Food to Avoid

Pulses   : Bengal gram, black gram, red beans

Vegetables : Peas, potato, cauliflower, sweet potato, colocasia, lady's finger, tomato, spinach, radish, cucumber

Fruits : Banana, pineapple, orange, guava, watermelon, muskmelon, mulberry, lemon, *phalsa* (*Grewia subinequalis*)

Drinks : Butter-milk, curd mixed with water, cold syrups, lime water

Cardiac diseases

Food to Eat

Grains : Old rice, barley, great millet, wheat

Pulses : Green gram, lentil, red gram

Vegetables : Snake gourd, spinach, fenugreek, bitter gourd, bottle gourd, radish

Fruits : Mango, pomegranate, papaya, apple, grapes, sapota

Drinks : Cow's milk, vinegar, honey, butter-milk, sesame oil

Rock salt, old jaggery, dry ginger, thyme, garlic, coriander, ginger, betel leaf, ash gourd are especially beneficial.

Food to Avoid

Pulses : Black gram, bengal gram

Vegetables : Cauliflower, potato, tomato, greean peas

Fruits : Banana

Avoid oils

Antagonistic Diet

Harmful Combinations of Food
There exist a good number of food stuffs in routine dietetics regimen, which if taken together, behave antagonistically and produce toxic effects in the body. Such combinations in Ayurveda are known as *Viruddha Aahar*. A few such combinations are:

- Milk with fish.
- Honey and ghee (in equal quantities).
- Milk — with radish, garlic, menthol or barley.
- Jack fruit — with black gram, jaggery and ghee.

- Milk — with raw mango, lemon, banana, rose apple, plum, Indian jujuba, pineapple, tamarind, and groundnut.
- *Kheer* (milk cooked with sugar and rice) with butter-milk.
- Honey with hot water.
- Cream with citrus fruit.
- Hot and cold things together.
- Milk with watermelon.
- Hot snacks with curd and tamarind chutney, together.
- Milk with salt or curd.
- Wine with rice cooked in milk and mixture of rice, pulses and condiments boiled together.
- Milk with sesame and jaggery.

Fasting

Ayurveda says fasting is the best medicine of all. It also says that fasting is very helpful in both mental and physical problems. There is a particular method for keeping fasts. In Ayurveda, rules and methods of fasting have been explained in details.

In normal healthy condition also, one should keep fasts, to maintain one's health, as it helps in purifying the gastro-intestinal tract and the surrounding organs. It normalises the metabolic components. It also increases the appetite and gives rest to the small and large intestines.

Types

1) Total Fasting: In this, one should not take anything.
2) On Liquids: One can take only liquids like milk, juice, coconut water etc.
3) On Fruits and Vegetables: One can take preparations which are made from vegetables and fruits only.

Apart from this, fasting can also help in certain diseased conditions. In such conditions one should keep a fast only after consulting a physician.

In this present era, people are more involved in materialistic things and are forgetting the Ayurvedic guidelines for achieving total health. Therefore, I hope that this small effort will provide some basic important guidelines to achieve holistic health.

Other titles in the series

- Sun Therapy

- Magnetotherapy

- Yoga

- Healing Powers of Water

- Fitness

- Kidney Stones

- Menopause

- Chronic Bronchitis

- HIV and AIDS

- Diabetes

- Typhoid

- Anxiety